LIVE THE ABUNDANT LIFE

Moving Beyond Our Pain

Melvina E. Dilosa

Copyright © 2014 by Melvina E.Dilosa

Live the Abundant Life
Moving Beyond Our Pain
by Melvina E.Dilosa

Printed in the United States of America

ISBN 9781629526966

All rights reserved solely by the author. The author guarantees all contents are original and do not infringe upon the legal rights of any other person or work. No part of this book may be reproduced in any form without the permission of the author. The views expressed in this book are not necessarily those of the publisher.

Scripture quotations taken from the King James Version (KJV) – public domain

Artwork: Edward Jones & Emanuel M. Dilosa

dilosa8485@yahoo.com

www.xulonpress.com

TABLE OF CONTENTS

Acknowledgments vii
Introduction ix
How to Use This Manual xi

PHASE I

Five-Part Makeup Of Mankind 15
Baggage Carriers 17
Pride 21
Defense Walls 25
Fears 29
Talking Walls 32
Beware Of Memory Lane 40
Anger Landmines 45

PHASE II

Transformation 51
Challenge Of Change 52
Mental Processing 53
Wholeness 55
Five-Part Spiritual Development 57
Humility 59
A New Heart 61
Tearing Down Walls 63
Silencing Voices 66

Avoiding Memory Lane 68
Principles For Anger Management 71
Graveyard Of Dead Issues 72
Peace Of God 77

Acknowledgments

To my husband, Rockne, my Pastor and my best friend—thank you for your encouragement, patience, support, and prayers. Thank you for not feeling threatened by the gifts God placed in me. I love you for teaching me the importance of balance when I became engrossed in my work. You have shown me how to love people God's way. Special thanks to my children for believing in me and listening to me relentlessly talk about "BAL"; I love you dearly. I thank God for my parents who provided a loving and safe environment and teaching me to be responsible and strong, most of all for planting the seed to believe in God at an early age.. To my Bibleway family thank you for your love, support and encouragement throughout the years God bless you. Most important I thank God for loving me with His prefect love and fulfilling my life.

Introduction

From the disobedience of Adam mankind fell out of relationship with God which resulted in a daily struggle for mankind to live in harmony without the presence of God in their lives. Therefore we must be reconciled to God, our creator, through Jesus Christ that we may know His love for us and our designed purpose on earth. Before we can fulfill this divine purpose we must know what prevents us from experiencing the peace of God that surpasses all understanding according to Philippians 4:7. It is our thought process that prevents us from walking and living the abundant life that God has promised us in St. John 10:10. Once we learn how to effectively use the word of God in a practical way for daily living we can begin to overcome obstacles and be victorious people of God.

I was ready to accept the invitation and give God a chance with my life; my soul was weary from the endless search for true love and hope. Matthew 11:28-29 Jesus invites all who have grown weary from sin to come unto Him that He may give rest to their souls. In desperation to have my emptiness filled I surrendered my life to God. God desired an intimate relationship with me that I might experience the abundant life He promised in His word. I had to walk in obedience to His word and trust Him with my life.
I pray that you desire an intimate relationship with God and fight to not be bound by Satan's weapons of destruction but experience spiritual freedom granted through Christ.

STRATEGIES FOR GROWTH

BEFORE ONE'S PROBLEM
CAN BE UPROOTED,
ONE MUST FIRST
IDENTIFY THE CORE
OF THE PROBLEM

How to Use This Manual

First this manual will challenge you to be honest that you may identify your unhealthy mindsets, emotions and behaviors. This mental entrapment prevents us from a healthy lifestyle. Next, you will reflect on the questions that challenge you to make positive changes. Last, you will need God's help to transform your mind that you may experience a positive and balanced life. I pray that you are determined to win this spiritual warfare from the entrapment of spiritual bondage to spiritual freedom. The objectives are designed to:

- Identify your mental and emotional state
- Reflect the damaging effects from life experiences
- Challenge your thinking
- Renew your thinking

Reflections

As you begin to answer each question, you must ask yourself, "Do I want to experience the abundant life God has promised or do I just want to exist?" Reflections will allow you to read each question, stop, look within and honestly identify your thoughts, emotions and behaviors, which are the residuals from negative life experiences. These experiences impact our lives and can change our perceptions, and desires toward things. I believe many want change in their lives but lack knowledge of how to accomplish this need.

Our spiritual imprisonment is the result of our fleshly lust and desires continually wanting fulfillment yet never being satisfied. Proverbs 3:6 instructs believers to acknowledge God in all their ways for divine direction which includes being freed from spiritual prisons. This freedom comes when we no longer live to please ourselves, but live to please God.

PHASE I

Five-Part Makeup
Of Mankind

Our spiritual nature is the most significant, for it is the core of our five-part makeup. Our spirit is led by one of the two rulings spirits in the earth, either the Spirit of Light being God the Creator of the heavens and earth, our divine authority, who has given us His word as our spiritual compass to live a holy and righteous life unto him. The spirit of darkness, being an enemy of God tempts us with evil thoughts to commit unrighteous acts that are contrary to God's word. Satan's mission is to kill, steal and destroy mankind. St.John 10:10. Our **spirit** chooses one of the ruling spirits to follow and it directs our thoughts and establishes mind sets, which is our second makeup, the **mental.**

It is the determining factor of how we see ourselves, others and the world around us, which impacts our decision making. The third makeup is **emotions,** which is our feelings. Our feelings which abide in the heart are awakened when we entertain thoughts. Jeremiah 17:9 described the nature of the heart as deceitful above all things, and desperately wicked: who can know it? Romans 7:18 the Apostle Paul acknowledges "For I know that in me (that is, in my flesh,) dwelleth no good thing." Mark 7:21 says, "For from within, out of the heart of men, proceed evil thoughts, adulteries, fornications, murders". Mark 7:23 states, "All these evil things come from within, and defile the man." The fourth makeup is our **social** which is communication. We may hide thoughts and feeings from others, but often times our thoughts and desires are communicated through our behavior.

We must guard against negative self-talk messages, which have the greatest effect upon us. Proverbs 18:21 says, "Death and life are in the power of the tongue"... It is important to understand that our words carry power. All of the above affects our **physical** health, which is the fifth makeup. When we are constantly entertaining negative thoughts it prevents the mind from resting which causes mental stress resulting in high blood pressure, strokes, ulcers and heart attacks. But, when our thoughts are good, lovely, pure and honest it uplifts our spirit and promotes good health. Proverbs 17:22 says, "A merry heart doeth good like a medicine..."

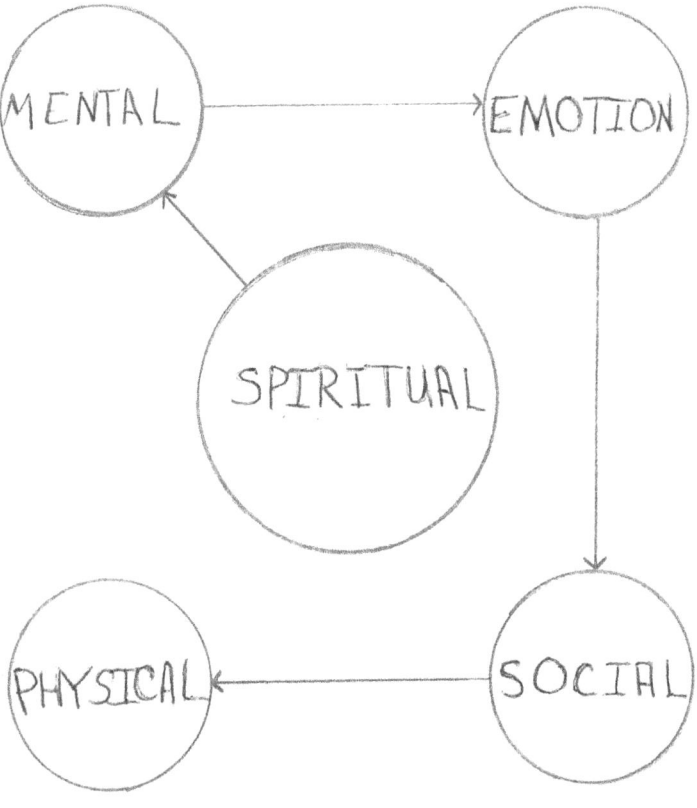

Baggage Carriers

Our baggage can help form our character

Our baggage is filled with negative mental and emotional residuals from life experiences.

Did you know that we gather baggage as early as childhood and can continue throughout life? Our baggage is filled with structured mindsets, warped imaginations, what we witness, hearsay, created perceptions and ill emotions all which are residuals from negative experiences in life. Unfortunately, we tend to hold onto unpleasant experiences that distort our thinking about life, family and society. Our growth often can be affected, which causes us to lose hope, miss opportunities, ruin relationships, harm others and ourselves, abandon dreams and cancels our future that we fail to fulfill our destined purpose in life.

In Matthew 11:28 Jesus says, "Come unto me, all ye that labor and are heavy laden, and I will give you rest." His invitation is for everyone with a troubled heart to surrender their baggage to Him.

Below fill your baggage with words that identify your unhealthy thoughts, feelings and behaviors.

> HOLDING ONTO PAIN
> GIVES US OWNERSHIP
> OF OUR BAGGAGE
> THAT WE REMAIN
> PRISONERS TO IT
>
> WE MUST CHOOSE
> TO DISCARD
> OUR BAGGAGE
> OR WE WILL
> CONTINUE TO CARRY
> A HEAVY HEART

BAGGAGE REFLECTION

We learn how to adjust to our baggage.

1. Name three negative thoughts in your baggage.

a) _____

(b) _____

(c) _____

2. Name three negative emotions in your baggage.

(a) _____

(b) _____

(c) _____

3. Name what in your baggage haunts you.

(a) _____

(b) _____

(c) _____

4. Name three benefits from releasing your baggage.

(a) _____

(b) _____

(c) _____

BAGGAGE = BONDAGE

Our baggage carries our identity which:

- Burdens the spirit

- Pollutes the mind
- Saddens the heart
- Destroys relationships.

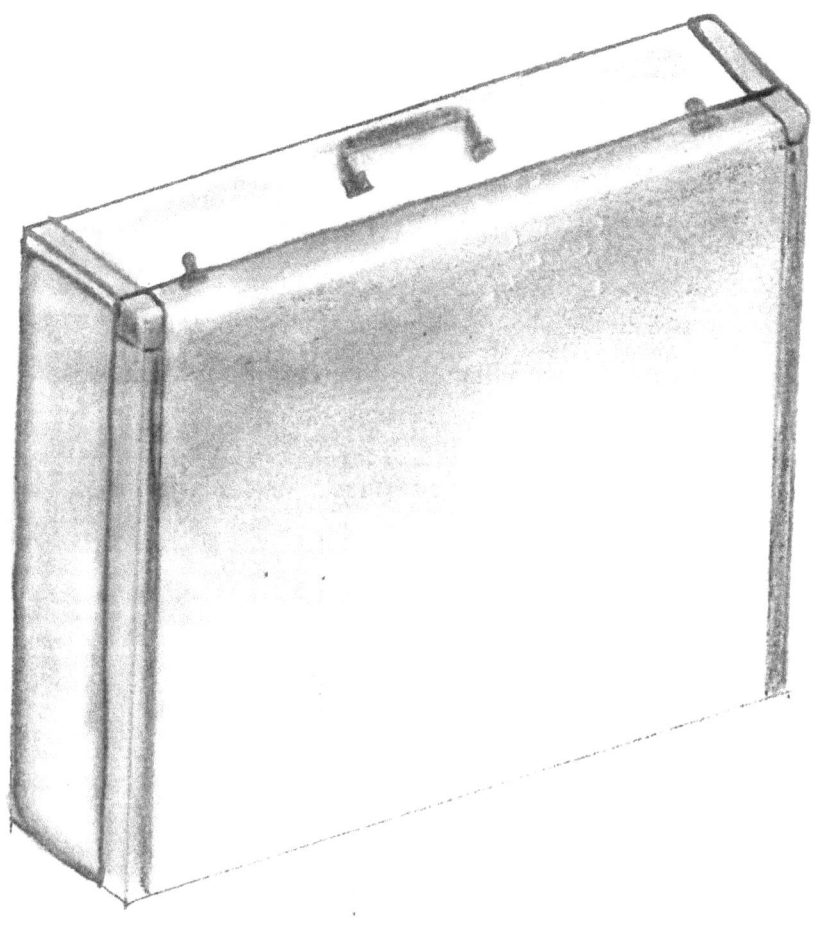

Pride

Pride is an enemy of humility

Pride is the handle of our baggage that carries the residuals from past life experiences; it is the influence factor of our choices, behavior and the cause for many of the problems in our lives. Pride is an evil spirit and the enemy of our souls. It deceives the mind to not think soberly; it is being self-righteous, arrogant, and high-minded while judging others as inferior to themselves. Glory seekers are drunk in their minds, thinking, "It's the all about me." It is a self-centered attitude that keeps one in denial of his or her true person, therefore, mental, emotional and social growth is delayed. Being self-centered disregards the acknowledgement of talents, potential or contributions of others. Self-centered people also fail to give God his due honor for enabling them with knowledge and gifts to perform and excel. Meanwhile others express their gratitude to God for their accomplishments, but they fall short of what God requires from them, which is a life devoted to His glory and not theirs. Pride is the handle of our baggage that keeps us a prisoner to unhealthy thoughts and past experiences.

The wicked, through the pride of his countenance, will not seek after God…Psalm 10: 4.

PRIDE
GOETH BEFORE
DESTRUCTION
AND A
HAUGHTY SPIRIT
BEFORE A FALL

PROVERBS 16:18

A MAN'S PRIDE
SHALL BRING HIM LOW:
BUT HONOR
SHALL UPHOLD
THE HUMBLE IN SPIRIT

PROVERBS 29:23

PRIDE REFLECTION

Pride is the handle of our baggage that keeps us in denial and destroys relationships

1. Name three prideful thoughts in your baggage.

(a) _____

(b) _____

(c) _____

2. Name three prideful emotions in your baggage.

(a) _____

(b) _____

(c) _____

3. Name three prideful acts that damage your relationships.

(a) _____

(b) _____

(c) _____

4. Explain why pride can be harmful to you.

(a) _____

(b) _____

(c) _____

PRIDE = BONDAGE

Pride keeps us a prisoner which:

- Imprisons the soul
- Destroys lives
- Severs relationships
- Devalues others

DEFENSE WALLS

Defense walls isolate us from receiving help

It was from my baggage that I built walls to protect myself from being hurt again. My perception about love and the disappointments in life had impacted my thinking and hardened my heart. Unfortunately, my experiences left mental and emotional residue that pushed me into a survival mode to build defense barriers. These barriers I call "Defense Walls". No one escapes from being a victim of life's troubles. Our negative experiences can leave an impact of painful memories that births anger, resentment, bitterness, abandonment, anxiety, fear, hurt, pain, guilt, shame, disappointment, remorse, and depression.

God revealed to me that Satan had deceived me to build walls for protection, but I was unaware that I had carried my pain behind the walls. Now, these walls isolated me and the past memories I constantly entertained only magnified the pain. The plan of Satan was to isolate me and taunt me continually to destroy my mind and life; the most frightening part was that I didn't even know where to start to bring them down!

…because fear hath torment… I John 4:18

Live the Abundant Life

I BUILT WALLS
TO PROTECT MYSELF
FROM FUTURE HURTS
BUT INSTEAD
I IMPRISONED MYSELF
WHICH ONLY
MAGNIFIED
MY PAIN

SATAN HAD DECEIVED
ME INTO BELIEVING
THAT I CREATED THE
IDEA TO BUILD
PROTECTION WALLS
BUT HIS PLAN
WAS TO ISOLATE ME
AND DESTROY MY MIND

DEFENSE WALLS REFLECTION

We live behind layers of walls for protection.

1. How have your walls affected your behavior?

(a) _____

(b) _____

(c) _____

2. How have your walls affected your relationships?

(a) _____

(b) _____

(c) _____

3. Name negative results from your isolation walls.

(a) _____

(b) _____

(c) _____

4. How will you build new relationships?

(a) _____

(b) _____

(c) _____

DEFENSE WALLS = BONDAGE

Our walls of protection may become our prison which:
- Imprisons the spirit
- Torments the mind
- Magnifies the pain
- Isolates relationships

Fears

Fear is an enemy of faith

Fear is a spirit and a weapon that Satan uses to control us. His plan was to destroy me through fear. At the age of twelve, I experienced my mother having a nervous breakdown which left me confused unable to comprehend what happen to her. The loving nurturing mother I knew suddenly became distant she no longer ate dinner with us but instead went to the basement talking out loud to invisible people and being totally consumed in her own world.

My father tried his best to explain my mother's sudden change of behavior, but I was too young to understand. As I became older, I often wondered if I would have a breakdown like my mother. I kept this fear to myself, then one day I read in my health and safety text book that mental illness was not hereditary.

I remember feeling relieved and fear leaving my mind. Later in life I learned that God gave me the answer, I so desperately needed as a child, to destroy the fear Satan was trying to plant in my spirit.

As I grew older the sin in my life caused me to experience more hurt and disappointments, and the fear of being hurt again convinced me to develop weapons to protect myself (Satan deceived me to believe my weapons would protect me from future hurts) but those even failed. Finally, I acknowledged that I needed a change in my life and surrendered my life to Christ. But when He allowed me to experience hurt again I was disillusioned and wanted to revert to using my former weapons. Then God told me, "Surrender all your weapons to me" fear came over me I felt I would be defenseless. The thought that I no longer would be in control of protecting myself frightened me. At that moment I realized I did not totally trust God with my life. I knew to please God I had to surrender all my plans and submit to His will. Hebrews 11:6 says, "But without faith it is impossible to please him: for he that cometh to God must believe that he is, and that he is a rewarder of them that diligently seek him". When we believe in God's word we trust Him and believe He has our best interest at heart and rest in the promise, "I WILL NEVER LEAVE THEE, NOR FORSAKE THEE"...Hebrews 13:5.

When we experience hurt, disappointment, abandonment and pain it provokes us to devise defense weapons to protect ourselves from being hurt again. But it is impossible to avoid unpleasant experiences for they are a part of life. King David proclaimed in Psalm 62:6, "He only is my rock and my salvation: he is my defence; I shall not be moved (shaken)." God's promises strengthens our faith to face challenges with courage.

EFFECTS OF FEAR = BONDAGE

Fear will keep us from experiencing God's plan for our life

- Cause us to procrastinate
- Makes us indecisive
- Gives us poor self-image
- Breeds negative thoughts
- Paralyzes us
- Avoids challenges
- Steals our peace
- Kills visions
- Destroys dreams
- Smothers ambitions
- Bombards the mind

Talking Walls

Spiritual warfare begins in the mind

Are you a person who always is thinking, daydreaming, imagining, being consumed with ideas, thoughts, and plans both positive and negative? This was how I spent a lot of time throughout my childhood years; for me it was a place of relaxation. As I grew older I practiced the same behavior. I dwelled more on the negative which resulted in a lot of time and energy wasted; being consumed in mental feedback with thoughts Satan or my flesh nature presented.

It is imperative that we walk guard duty over our minds and watch the thoughts we entertain, or the peace which God has granted us will be disturbed or stolen. God revealed to me that Satan tempted me with two mental messages, "Remember When..." and What If..." to trouble my spirit. Even though Satan had no power over my mind the unforgiveness in my heart allowed him to hold me captive to anger, resentment, bitterness and hostility. St. John 8:36 says, "If the Son therefore shall make you free, ye shall be free indeed". Before I could be free I had to be willing to forgive others and allow God to heal my wounded heart from unforgiveness.

True freedom comes when there is a transformation in our thinking and it no longer matters what someone said or did to us. It is critical that we monitor our thoughts and ask God to balance our thinking or our minds will run wild with imaginations that cause negative emotions and behaviors. ...forgetting those things which are behind... Philippians 3:13

SATAN'S STRATEGY
WAS TO
DESTROY ME
THROUGH
NEGATIVE MESSAGES
ABOUT MY
PAST EXPERIENCES

SATAN PRESENTS
"REMEMBER WHEN"
TO REMINDS US
OF OUR PAST
WHICH CANNOT
BE CHANGED

TALKING WALLS REFLECTION

We must resist Satan's distorted messages.

1. Name "Remember When" thoughts.

   (a) _____

   (b) _____

   (c) _____

2. Name emotional effects from "Remember When" thoughts.

   (a) _____

   (b) _____

   (c) _____

3. Issues I need to release.

   (a) _____

   (b) _____

   (c) _____

4. Areas where I need to move on.

(a) _____

(b) _____

(c) _____

SATAN'S STRATEGY
WAS TO
DESTROY ME
THROUGH
NEGATIVE MESSAGES
CONCERNING MY
FUTURE

SATAN PRESENTS
"WHAT IF"
TO MAKE ME ANXIOUS
ABOUT THE FUTURE

TALKING WALLS REFLECTION

We need to ask God to balance our thinking.

1. Name "What If" thoughts.

   (a) _____

   (b) _____

   (c) _____

2. Name the emotional effects from "What If" thoughts.

   (a) _____

   (b) _____

   (c) _____

3. Areas where I worry about my future.

   (a) _____

   (b) _____

   (c) _____

4. Thoughts I think about too much.

(a) _____

(b) _____

(c) _____

TALKING WALLS = BONDAGE

Talking walls tempt us to dwell on our past and worry about our future which:

- Troubles the spirit
- Tempts the mind
- Condemns the heart
- Poisons relationships

BEWARE OF SATAN'S WEAPONS

His plan is to destroy mankind

- Guilt
- Shame
- Regrets
- Hurts
- Fears
- Snapshot memories

- Negative mental messages
- Temptations
- False Accusations

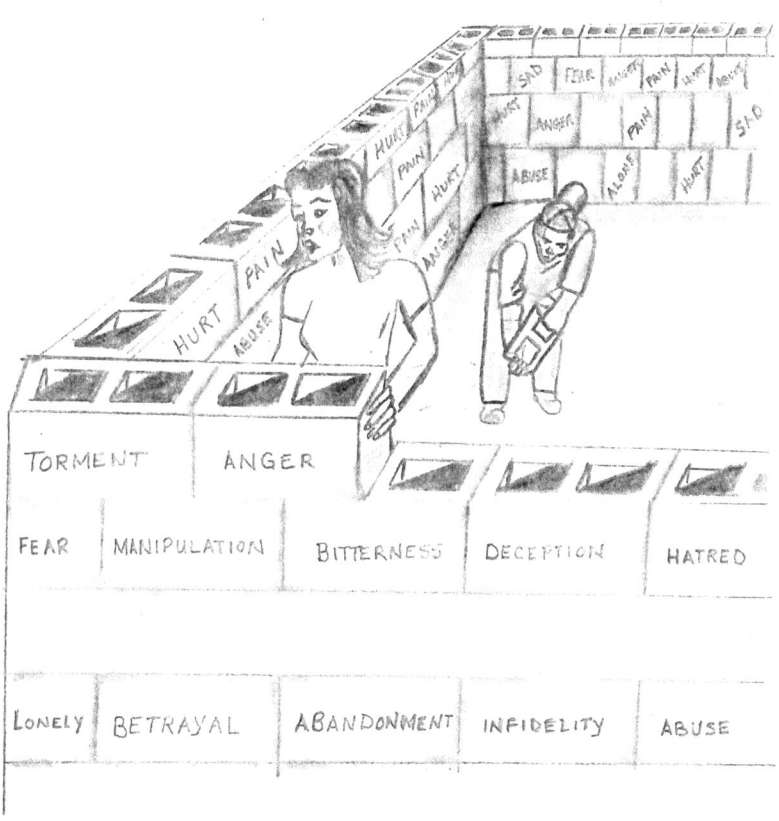

Beware Of Memory Lane

Refuse to dwell on bad experiences from your past

Resist the temptation to revisit past hurts that Satan presents to your mind, for he is a strategist whose mission is to kill, steal and destroy mankind…St. John 10:10. Satan continually reminded me about painful experiences of my past, which made me feel justified and entitled to hold grudges which kept me bitter, but unaware of its damaging effects. Even though I had the power to resist Satan my flesh nature wanted to entertain his messages which lured me back into Memory Lane. He deceived me to feel comfortable in a place which only held painful memories.

When I no longer could endure the pain caused by unforgiveness I asked God to free me. One night God awakened me with a vision showing Satan reminding me about past experiences as we walked down a long cobble stone path. God said, "Satan reminds you of past offenses and each time you entertain the thoughts PAIN, HURT and FEAR resurrects in you." These words also appeared on the bricked path.

Then God showed Satan leaving me after he accomplished his goal to wound my heart. In this dream I remember feeling numb, helpless, betrayed and abandoned. Then, afar off I saw Jesus coming down the path to rescue me. I was ashamed for being disobedient and listening to Satan which caused me to be to his victim. Later God told me, "You were vulnerable to Satan's attacks because you had unforgiveness in your heart." I never realized the power and self-destruction of unforgiveness.

THROUGH A VISION
GOD REVEALED
THAT REVISITING
MEMORY LANE
WILL ALWAYS RESURRECT
PAIN, HURT AND FEAR

MEMORY LANE REFLECTION

Unforgiveness imprisons our spirit.

1. Why I feel entitled to get revenge.

(a) _____

(b) _____

(c) _____

2. How does revenge benefit or remove your pain?

(a) _____

(b) _____

(c) _____

3. Name unforgiveness issues that haunt you.

(a) _____

(b) _____

(c) _____

4. What I enjoy about dwelling on my past experiences.

(a) _____

(b) _____

(c) _____

MEMORY LANE = BONDAGE

Memory Lane reopens old wounds which:

- Grieves the spirit
- Revives old memories
- Resurrects past hurts
- Destroys healthy relationships

PAST OFFENSES
WAS
SATAN'S BAIT
AND
UNFORGIVENESS
WAS
THE HOOK
THAT KEPT ME
A PRISONER TO MY PAIN

UNFORGIVENESS
WILL ALWAYS
LURE US
BACK INTO
MEMORY LANE

GOD TOLD ME,
"STOP NURSING YOUR WOUNDS".

I WAS UNAWARE
OF THE EMOTIONAL EFFECT
FROM ENTERTAINING THOUGHTS
ABOUT PAST EXPERIENCES

Anger Landmines

Holding anger is a choice

Everyone will experience anger at one time or another, but how we release it is the problem. Ephesians 4:26 says, "Be ye angry, and sin not:: let not the sun go down upon your wrath". When we continually think negative and hold to unpleasant experiences it can cause us to stay angry and unable to live peaceably with others. When we harbor anger it becomes a root of bitterness that poisons the mind with negative thinking and prevents us from having healthy relationships.

My choice to stay angry grew into bitterness which imprisoned my spirit, destroyed my inner peace and made me a prisoner to my pain. People who lack self-control respond out of impulse, react out of rage and cause harm to themselves and others. When we discipline our emotions it keeps us from escalating and losing control. It is imperative that we learn and practice positive alternatives to avoid grief and pain. God empowers us through the Holy Spirit with godly wisdom to control our emotions when we become angry.

A soft answer turneth away wrath: but grievous words stir up anger…Proverbs 15:1

GOD TOLD ME,
"AS LONG
AS YOU
BLAME
YOU WILL
CONTINUE
TO HURT"

WHEN GOD
TOLD ME I
COULDN'T
GET MY
LICK BACK
I FELT CHEATED

ANGER REFLECTIONS

Holding anger can grow into a root of bitterness

1. Name thoughts that birth anger.

   (a) _____

   (b) _____

   (c) _____

2. How has anger affected your relationships?

   (a) _____

   (b) _____

   (c) _____

3. Name losses you have experienced from anger.

   (a) _____

   (b) _____

   (c) _____

4. Name the rewards for remaining calm.

(a) _____

(b) _____

(c) _____

ANGER LANDMINES = BONDAGE

Anger can cause us to lose focus and react out of impulse which:

- Disrupts the spirit
- Troubles the mind
- Arouses emotions
- Attacks others

PHASE II

Transformation

And be not conformed to this world: but be ye transformed by the renewing of your mind…Romans 12: 2

I Corinthians 2:14 states, "But the natural man receiveth not the things of the Spirit of God: for they are foolishness unto him: neither can he know them, because they are spiritually discerned. I was trying to understand the ways of God through intellect and reasoning but I needed a mind renewal if I was to understand the mind and heart of God. I learned that God desires intimacy that I might know and experience His awesome love for me. Transformation is an ongoing process throughout our spiritual walk. It means denying our flesh its sinful pleasures and obeying the word of God that our spiritual man may be strengthened. Draw nigh to God, and He will draw nigh to you…James 4:8

> AND BE RENEWED
> IN THE SPIRIT
> OF YOUR MIND
>
> EPHESIANS 4:23

CHALLENGE OF CHANGE

Therefore, if any man be in Christ, he is a new creature: old things are passed away; behold, all things are become new…I Corinthians 5:17

- Change challenges the norm
- Change means leaving our comfort zone
- Change means being honest with myself
- Change is adopting positive mindsets
- Change is having a new perspective
- Change means working on self
- Change means changing negative self-talk
- Change comes through self-discipline
- Change is accepting new and positive methods
- Change means changing negative associates
- Change can make us fearful of the unknown
- Change means being a doer of the word of God
- Change is living a Christ-centered life

Mental Processing

Wherefore gird up the loins of your mind, be sober... I Peter 1:13

The processing stage is where we engage in spiritual warfare to destroy established mindsets and distorted perceptions that our mind may transform to the mind of Christ. This metamorphosis of the mind is known as processing. In times of trouble our faith is challenged to trust God and stay obedient to His word that others may witness Christ in our lives. Our inner battle is the flesh nature (carnal) fighting against the godly nature, which desires to please God. Unfortunately, in the processing stage many believers lose hope and faith in God while others validate their faith and remain committed to His commandments.

Philippians 2:5 says, "Let this mind be in you which was also in Christ Jesus." His desire was to do the will do the Father. Romans 12: 2 says, "And be not conformed this world: but be ye transformed by the renewing of your mind..." The believer (who is a new spiritual man created after God) needs a mind transformation to understand the mind of God.

Ephesians 4:23-24 instructs us to be renewed in the spirit of our mind and put on the character of God.

... THE CARNAL MIND
IS ENMITY
AGAINST GOD...

ROMANS 8:7

FOR THAT WHICH
I DO I ALLOW NOT:
FOR WHAT I WOULD,
THAT DO I NOT;
BUT WHAT I HATE,
THAT DO I.

ROMANS 7:15-19

Wholeness

We are complete in Him…Colossians 2:10

Before salvation I was going through life making choices from intuitions, hearsay and limited knowledge based on past experiences. Once I came into a relationship with God, my Creator, my spirit man came alive through God, filling my emptiness and making me whole. Now I trust in God's wisdom to lead my life for He is omniscience (all knowing) and has proven that He has my best interest at heart. He instructs me in Proverbs 3:5-6 to trust in Him with all my heart and no longer trust in my own judgment but acknowledge Him in my decision making that He may direct my path. I am His responsibility.

God has healed past hurts, pain and fears and continually delivers my soul from mental, emotional and spiritual prisons created by Satan. Now I honor God by living a devoted life unto Him for He has made me whole and given my life meaning. When we believe God loves us, we have a new perspective to value ourselves, others and respect nature.

God's desire for mankind is to know that there is completeness in His love for without His presence in our lives we will continue to search for completeness in the wrong persons, places and things hoping to fill the void.

KNOWING OUR DIVINE PURPOSE IN GOD ESTABLISHES OUR VALUE

FIVE-PART SPIRITUAL DEVELOPMENT

As we come into a relationship with God our spiritual man begins to develop. 2 Corinthians 5: 17 says, "Therefore if any man be in Christ, he is a new creature: old things are passed away; behold, all things are become new." Ephesians 4:23 says, be renewed in the spirit of your mind, this conversion allows the Spirit of God to give us insight about the nature of God, and what is required as followers of Christ. We dedicate our bodies as a living sacrifice that must be holy and acceptable unto God…Romans 12:1. Our body is the temple, the dwelling place, for the Spirit of God…I Corinthians 6:19. God's Spirit in us is the core part of our five-part development that guides us in all truth …St. John 16:13

SPIRITUAL

- Reveals that we are valuable …Psalm 139:14
- Guides us in all truth…St. John 16:13
- Brings us peace beyond natural understanding… Philippians 4:7
- Directs us how to be sons and daughters of God… Romans 8:14

MENTAL

- Renews the spirit of our mind …Ephesians 4:23

- Teaches us how to think… Philippians 4:8
- Transforms us by the renewing of our minds… Romans 12:2
- Desires the mind of Christ…Philippians 2:5

EMOTIONAL

- Describes the nature of the heart as desperately wicked… Jeremiah 17:9
- Deceives us with false feelings…Proverbs 14:12
- Expresses that a merry heart makes a cheerful countenance… Proverbs 15:13
- Reveals that by sorrow of the heart the spirit is broken… Proverbs 15:13

SOCIAL

- Honors God through praise and worship…Psalms 34:1
- Esteems others…Philippians 2:3
- Expresses the power of our words …Proverbs 18:21
- Instructs us how to live peaceably with all men… Romans 12:18

PHYSICAL

- Satisfies the longing soul…Psalm 107:9
- A merry heart is good like a medicine… Proverbs 17:22
- A broken spirit dries the bones… Proverbs 17:22
- Anger rests in the bosom of fools… Ecclesiastes 7:9

HUMILITY

"Before destruction the heart of man is haughty; and before honor is humility"…Proverbs 18:12

I experienced humility the day I admitted to myself, "It's gotta get better than this!" The pleasures of sin left me disappointed and empty, I wanted to experience real love and to have a hope. In my spirit I felt there was more for me in life and a reason for my existence beside pain, sorrow and death. My troubled spirit brought me to a place of humility to surrender my life and give God a chance to fill the void. Humility allows us to be honest with ourselves, others and admit to our shortcomings (faults, weaknesses, failures). We must be willing to challenge ourselves if we desire better communication in our relationships and marriages.

Pride, being the opposite of humility, causes us to stay in denial and blame others rather than acknowledge the truth about ourselves. This spirit God hates because it prevents us from having an intimate relationship with Him.

In times of adversity we must have the humility of Christ that others may witness the presence of Christ in our lives.

Proverbs 29:23 says, "A man's pride shall bring him low: but honor shall uphold the humble in spirit.

THE FEAR OF THE LORD
IS THE INSTRUCTION OF WISDOM;
AND BEFORE HONOUR IS HUMILITY
...PROVERBS 15:33

A New Heart

"Create in me a clean heart, O God; and renew a right spirit within me"...Psalm 51:10.

We need the heart of Christ that we may walk in humility

BLESSED ARE THE
PURE IN HEART:
FOR THEY
SHALL SEE GOD

MATTHEW 5:8

A NEW HEART

...Thou shalt love the Lord thy God with all thy heart...Luke 10:27

- Lifts the spirit
- Cleanses the mind
- Lightens the heart
- Builds relationships

I no longer wanted to live to fulfill the lust of my flesh (Galatians 5:19-21; I Corinthians 6:9) now my heart desired to please God by keeping His commandments and loving others. Finally my life is complete because I live a holy and righteous life unto Him. As God continues to free me from prisons of my past I continue to worship, praise and give Him honor for rescuing me from a life of sin.

TEARING DOWN WALLS

"Ye that fear the Lord, trust in the Lord: he is their help and their shield"…Psalm 115:11

Prior to salvation I experienced hurts and disappointments that pushed me to build walls for protection. I was suspicious of people and kept them at a distance to discern their intentions and actions. I built defense walls out of fear. My pride did not want to admit it was fear because it meant I was weak. The walls had imprisoned me with a false sense of security. Satan continually talked about past hurts which magnified the pain and tormented me. My mind was tired of thinking about past pains and my soul needed rest. I wanted to escape but had no clue how to bring down my walls.

Once I surrendered my life to God He began to work on the areas where I lacked faith. My faith was challenged when He told me, "Surrender all your weapons to me." He was asking me to let down my defense walls, surrender all my weapons and trust Him to take care of me. The thought that God might allow me to suffer the same hurts again caused me to fear there was an inner war to either walk in faith or keep a plan B for protection. Eventually my faith grew to surrender my weapons. In spite of new hurts God continues to heal my heart, keep my sanity and protect me from being destroyed by Satan's attacks.

Faith in God means believing He loves us with a perfect love, has our best interest at heart and will not allow anything or anyone to destroy us. We will suffer hurts in our spiritual walk but God has promised to sustain us, never leave or forsake us (Hebrews 13:5).

God will heal every hurt and take away painful memories (when we ask Him) that we may rest in His protection…Isaiah 54:17

Tearing Down Walls

…AND DELIVERED
ME FROM ALL
MY FEARS
…PSALM 34:4

TEARING DOWN DEFENSE WALLS

"My defence is of God, which saveth the upright in heart"... Psalm 7:10.

- Frees the spirit
- Rests the mind
- Releases fear
- Strengthens our faith

SILENCING VOICES

"Casting down imaginations, and every high thing that exalteth itself against the knowledge of God…" 2 Corinthians 10:5.

The moment we awaken and throughout our day we choose whether we will entertain positive or negative thoughts. We have no control over the thoughts presented to our minds (through our flesh nature or Satan) but we are in control of which ones we will entertain. We can make wiser choices when we understand the connection between our thoughts and emotions. Dwelling on negative thoughts can arouse negative emotions and unhealthy behaviors. Sometimes thoughts about offences press our minds to continually rehearse what transpired until we are consumed with anxiety, fear, anger, doubt, etc. We must watch the unsafe places where our minds wander to avoid opening our spirit to commit ungodly and harmful acts toward ourselves or others.

In this spiritual warfare God has empowered us to resist and cast down the imaginations Satan presents to us that we may escape being his victim…James 4:7 The Apostle Paul teaches in Philippians 4:8-9 what we are to think on that our mind and spirit may rest in His peace…Isaiah 26:3.

Silencing Voices

SUBMIT YOURSELVES THEREFORE TO GOD.
RESIST THE DEVIL,
AND SATAN WILL FLEE
FROM YOU
...JAMES 4:7

SILENCING VOICES

"Thou wilt keep him in perfect peace, whose mind is stayed on thee: because he trusteth in thee". Isaiah 26:3.

- Gives consolation to our spirit
- Settles the heart
- Builds hope
- Decreases daydreaming.

Avoiding Memory Lane

"Submit yourselves therefore to God. Resist the devil, and he will flee from you" James 4:7.

God revealed that unforgiveness held my heart captive to bitterness and vulnerable to Satan's messages. I realized to be free I had to forgive or continue being lured back to Memory Lane. I wrestled in making a decision because pride said, "I'm entitled to stay angry with you", "How dare you do that to me", "I have a right to stay bitter with you." Then God told me, "You don't want to forgive because you want your lick back! Let it go!" I felt cheated because holding grudges was my way of payback but I knew God wanted to free me from my pain, it was for my good.

Our flesh nature is negative and loves to keep our mind in the past but we must fight to not revisit Memory Lane, the path of darkness, which always resurrects past pain, hurt and fear. We must recognize the power and self-destruction of unforgiveness and quickly surrender our offenses and pains to God that our wounds may be healed and we avoid being a prisoner to our pain.

Philippians 3:13 instructs us to forget those things which are behind, and keep moving forward reaching for the goal to have an intimate relationship with God.

CASTING DOWN IMAGINATIONS, AND EVERY HIGH
THING THAT EXALTETH ITSELF AGAINST THE
KNOWLEDGE OF GOD, AND BRINGING INTO CAPTIVITY
EVERY THOUGHT TO THE OBEDIENCE OF CHRIST…
2 CORINTHIANS 10:5

AVOIDING MEMORY LANE

Brethren, I count not myself to have apprehended: but this one thing I do, forgetting those things which are behind, and reaching forth unto those things which are before...Philippians 3:13

- Revives old memories
- Resurrects hurt
- Resurrects pain
- Resurrects fear

Principles For Anger Management

He that is slow to anger is better than the mighty; and he that ruleth his spirit than he that taketh a city...Proverbs 16:32.

Anger can cause us to lose focus and respond out of impulse bringing harm to ourselves and others.

- Seek God for divine help.
- Put away anger.
- Choose to forgive.
- Consider the consequences.
- Know the danger of bitterness.
- Let go and move on.
- Refuse to nurse your wounds.
- Resist the temptation to stay bitter.
- Don't dwell on negative thoughts and past hurts.

GRAVEYARD OF DEAD ISSUES

"Therefore if any man be in Christ, he is a new creature: old things are passed away"... 2 Corinthians 5:17

One night God revealed through a vision my spiritual state He showed me a graveyard with its gate hanging off its hinges, weeds had overtaken the landscape and the tombstones were barely standing upright. The Lord said, "The things that keep you bitter are dead issues and you need to bury them." I was holding grudges, resentment, strife, evil thinking, hardness and insensitivity, which imprisoned my spirit from loving God's way. As I grew closer to God He continually worked with me to release everything that prevented me from enjoying the abundant life promised in His word (St John 10:10).

I wrestled with my flesh that wanted to stay spiritually bound to bitterness but even more I wanted His inner peace. In spite of my inner struggle I humbled myself and made the decision to forgive (as He so many times had forgiven me). When you become offended ask God for strength to release the hurts and heal your wounded heart that you may forgive and have the peace of God. Forgiveness carries the beautiful fragrance of Christ in our spirit that others may see His power, love and presence in our lives.

We must let the past pass away, bury bad memories and negative feelings if we want to live the abundant life.

I pray this manual has challenged you to let God start the healing process in your heart that you may continue to walk in the power and authority of God.

WE MUST CHOOSE
TO
BURY DEAD ISSUES
IN
OUR HEARTS

THE GRAVEYARD
ACKNOWLEDGES
THAT ALL MEMORIES
OF
HURTS, PAINS AND FEARS
HAVE BEEN BURIED

Graveyard

We bury our past to have a brighter future.

1. Name thoughts that need burying.

   (a) _____

   (b) _____

   (c) _____

2. Name thoughts that need burying.

   (a) _____

   (b) _____

   (c) _____

3. How did you grow as an individual from releasing your pain?

   (a) _____

   (b) _____

   (c) _____

4. Express how burying issues strengthened your relationships.

(a) _____

(b) _____

(c) _____

Graveyard Of Dead Issues

We will no longer carry the dead scent in our spirit from past hurts.

- Frees our spirits
- Cleanses the mind
- Lifts the heart
- Strengthens relationships

> THEREFORE IF ANY MAN
> BE IN CHRIST,
> HE IS
> A
> NEWCREATURE:
> OLD THINGS
> ARE PASSED AWAY;
> BEHOLD,
> ALL THINGS
> ARE BECOME NEW
> 2 CORINTHIANS 5:17

PEACE OF GOD

"Peace I leave with you, my peace I give unto you: not as the world giveth, give I unto unto… St. John 14:27

God's abiding presence is with us in the midst of our storms. He will quiet our spirit and settle our heart as we trust Him to bring us out with a strong arm…Isaiah 40:10

- Calms the spirit
- Quiets the mind
- Settles the heart
- Comforts the soul

www.ingramcontent.com/pod-product-compliance
Ingram Content Group UK Ltd.
Pitfield, Milton Keynes, MK11 3LW, UK
UKHW022220230426
12048UKWH00016BA/959